German
Russian
begin the
for the city
Stalingrad

Mu

Allies drop
tomic bombs
Japan surrenders
d the Pacific war.
Day (Victory over
Japan Day) is
15 August.

August 1942

May 1945

August 1945

Allies
desert bc
of El Alam
North A

northern
France.

Allied infantry
(soldiers on foot)
fighting in the desert

D0186814

BRENT LIBRARIES

Please return/renew this item
by the last date shown.
Books may also be renewed by
phone or online.
Tel: 0333 370 4700
On-line www.brent.gov.uk/libraryservice

91120000373607

Penguin Random House

Senior editor Marie Greenwood
Senior designer Ann Cannings
Jacket coordinator Francesca Young
Jacket designer Amy Keast, Suzena Sengupta
Managing editor Laura Gilbert
Managing art editor Diane Peyton Jones
Picture research Nishwan Rasool
Pre-production producer Dragana Puvacic
Producer Isabell Schart
Art director Martin Wilson
Publisher Sarah Larter
Publishing director Sophie Mitchell
Educational consultant Jacqueline Harris

Designed, edited and project-managed for DK by Dynamo Ltd.

First published in Great Britain in 2017 by
Dorling Kindersley Limited
80 Strand, London, WC2R 0RL

Copyright © 2017 Dorling Kindersley Limited
A Penguin Random House Company
10 9 8 7 6 5 4 3 2 1
001–299050–Sept/2017

All rights reserved.
No part of this publication may be reproduced, stored in or introduced into a retrieval system, or transmitted, in any form, or by any means (electronic, mechanical, photocopying, recording, or otherwise), without the prior written permission of the copyright owner.

A CIP catalogue record for this book is available from the British Library.
ISBN: 978-0-2412-8514-5

Printed and bound in Malaysia

A WORLD OF IDEAS:
SEE ALL THERE IS TO KNOW

www.dk.com

Contents

4 What led to World War II?

6 Rise of the Nazis

8 The children escape

10 War begins

12 Key players

14 Living with the enemy

16 Operation Dynamo

18 Wartime women

20 Battle of Britain

22 Propaganda

24 Wartime entertainment

BRENT LIBRARIES

91120000373607	
Askews & Holts	29-Jun-2018
J940.53	£5.99

26 Battles at sea

28 Animal heroes

30 Tanks into Russia

32 Air power

34 The Holocaust

36 Anne Frank

38 Desert warfare

40 Growing up in the war

42 Pearl Harbor

44 Wartime food

46 Code-breakers

48 D-Day

50 City bombings

52 War ends in Europe

54 Atomic bomb

56 After the war

58 World War II facts and figures

60 Glossary

62 Index

64 Acknowledgements

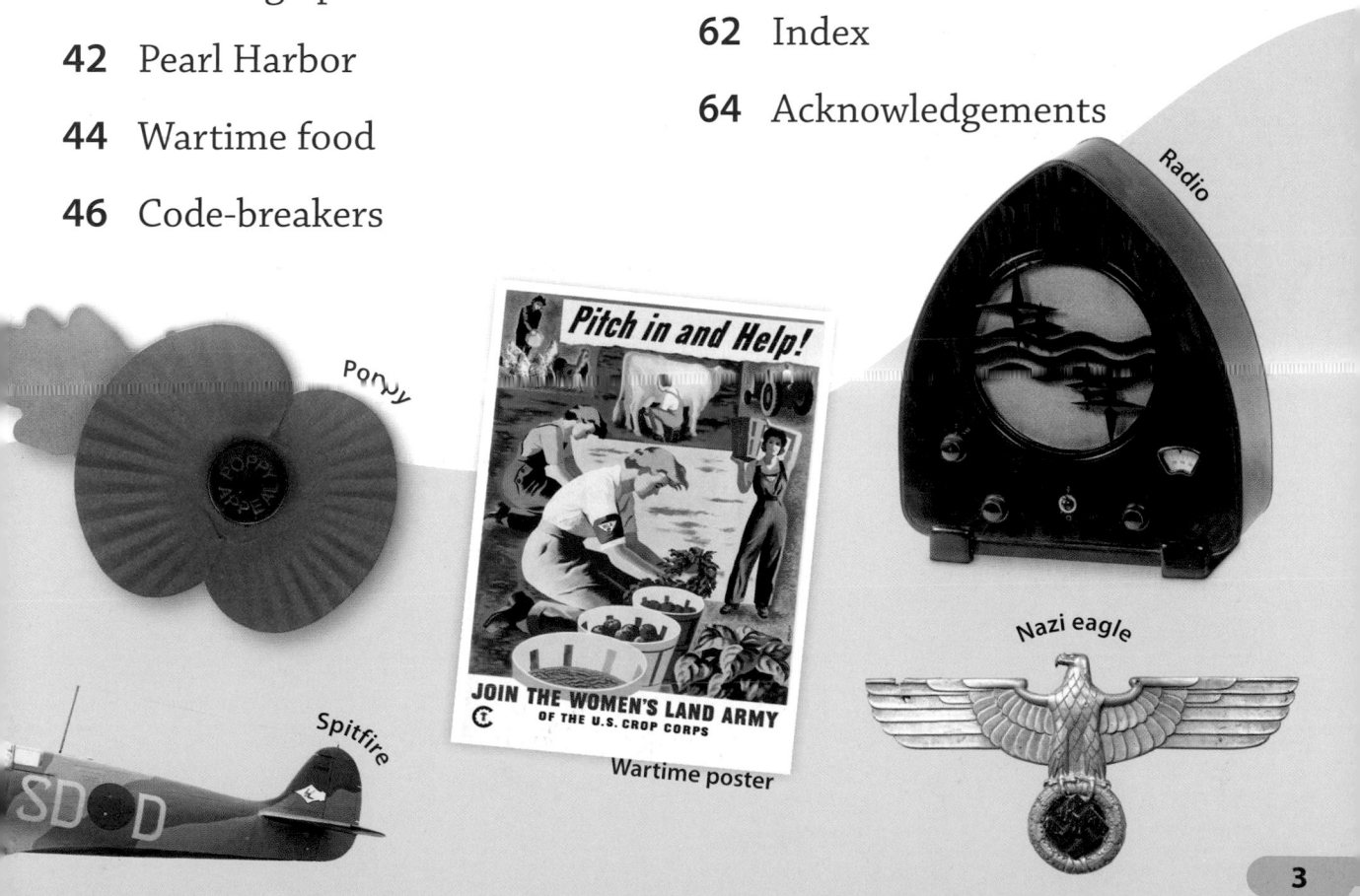

What led to World War II?

1918 World War I ends
World War I lasted from 1914 to 1918. Most of the fighting was in Europe and the Middle East. It is also called the Great War.

Hitler's rise to power after World War I paved the way for the largest, deadliest war in history. World War II lasted six years, and fighting spread across Europe into Africa, Asia, and the Pacific Islands.

1933 Hitler comes to power
The German people vote for the Nazi party and Adolf Hitler. Hitler vows to make Germany strong again, after its defeat in World War I.

1935 New weapons
Germany becomes more powerful. The country begins making new weapons, including bomber planes.

German Dornier Do 17 bomber

German army helmet

1936 Germany on the move
After World War I, German armed forces were not allowed in the Rhineland, a German region that bordered France. In March, 1936, German troops re-enter it.

German tanks
The Germans tested tanks in secret. They tried out their new Panzers, such as this PzKw II tank, in mock (pretend) battles.

1939 World War II begins
Europe had tried to avoid war by letting Hitler's army grow and take over other countries. This approach failed, as Hitler wanted more. In September 1939, Germany invades Poland.

1920s Money loses value
The world struggles after the war. The same amount of money buys less and less each day. The Germans, who had lost the war, suffer most.

Children playing with stacks of worthless German cash

Poppies
About 18 million people died in World War I. Today, people wear a poppy to remember those who died in all wars.

1930s No jobs, no money
The money crisis leads to banks closing all over the world. Factories close, too. Many people lose their jobs.

Jobless people marching in protest in England

Swastika
New leaders promised better times. Mussolini came to power in Italy. In Germany, Hitler made the swastika the flag of the new Nazi Party.

1937 Japan attacks China
China is weak, because of civil (internal) war. In July, Japan invades, seeing the chance to lead Asia and make a new empire.

Rising Sun Flag of Japan

1938 Takeovers
Hitler makes Austria part of Germany. He also takes hold of part of Czechoslovakia (what is now the Czech Republic and Slovakia).

! WOW!

Germany had **no air force** after 1918. New pilots learned by **flying gliders.**

Rise of the Nazis

Hard times followed World War I. Germany had lost the war and had to pay those who won. German money lost value and banks were forced to shut. Factories closed down. People lost jobs and hope. They turned to the Nazis, led by Adolf Hitler, who promised to make Germany great.

Hitler

Hitler became Germany's leader in 1933. His National Socialist Party was also known as the Nazis. Hitler stopped paying war damages and promised the German people new factories and roads. He also formed a new army and air force. He talked about a new German empire, or "Reich".

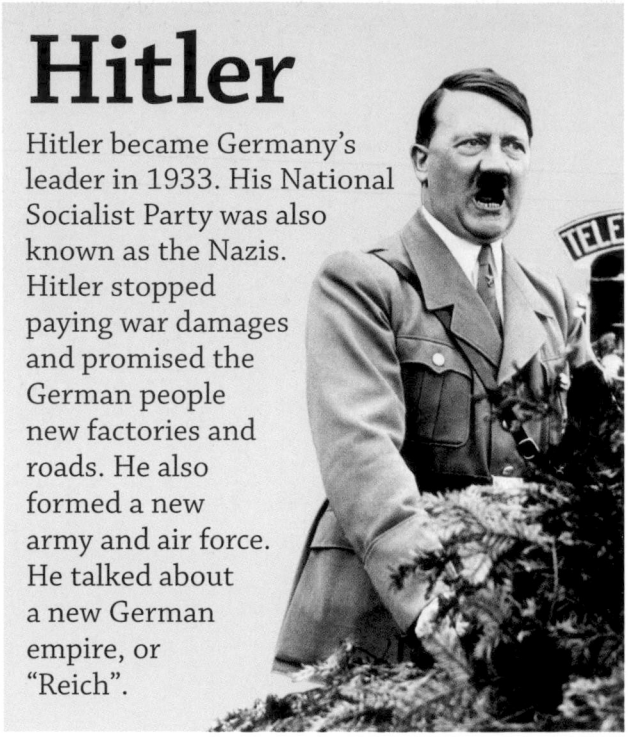

RALLIES

The Nazis punished anyone who spoke against them. They held huge rallies (public meetings) to whip up support. Bands played, banners waved, soldiers and children marched. Hitler roused the crowds with fiery speeches. He promised Germany would rule Europe.

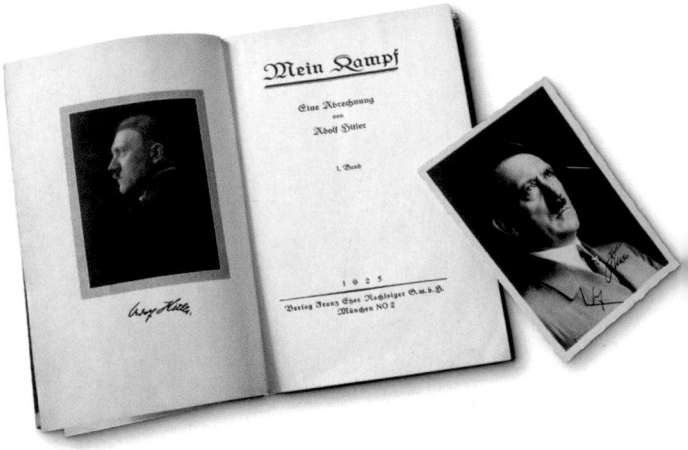

Hitler's ideas

Hitler was born in Austria. He joined Germany's army in World War I and led the Nazi Party from 1921. In 1924, he went to prison where he wrote *Mein Kampf* (My Struggle). This book blamed Jewish people and Communists for Germany's problems.

Nazi symbols

The Nazis put their symbols everywhere, on flags, uniforms, buildings, and even on schools. Their signs included this eagle and the swastika, an ancient cross. The Nazis used these badges to show everyone who ruled Germany. Just seeing these symbols made many people proud, but they scared others.

OLYMPICS

The 1936 Olympic Games took place in Berlin. The Nazis used the Games to show off. Crowds cheered every German winner. However, the star of the Games was US athlete Jesse Owens. He won three gold medals, and Hitler walked out. Why? Owens was an African-American. His success went against Nazi racist ideas.

Kristallnacht

On 9 November 1938, Nazi gangs trashed Jewish shops and attacked and killed many Jewish people. Nazis painted messages of hate on walls and doors. They threw petrol bombs. They set shops on fire and smashed windows. Shattered glass covered the streets. It was called *Kristallnacht*, or the "Night of Glass".

Children bravely began life in a strange land.

The children escape

After 1933, Jewish people lived in danger under Nazi rule. Many Jewish families sent their children away for safety. About 10,000 child refugees escaped to Britain. British children were also seeking shelter, for war seemed ever closer. They left city homes for the countryside, as evacuees.

Kindertransport

Kindertransport means "children's transport" in German. It was an escape plan for Jewish children to flee to Britain. They travelled by train and ship. Many were scared, not knowing what awaited them. They found new homes with British families. But many never saw their own families again.

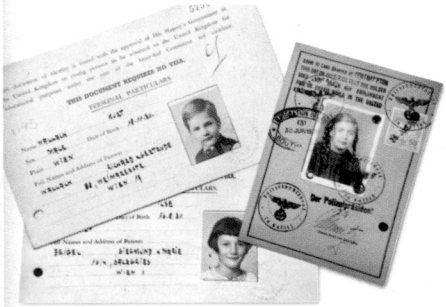

Refugee children needed travel passes called visas. British helpers got these for them.

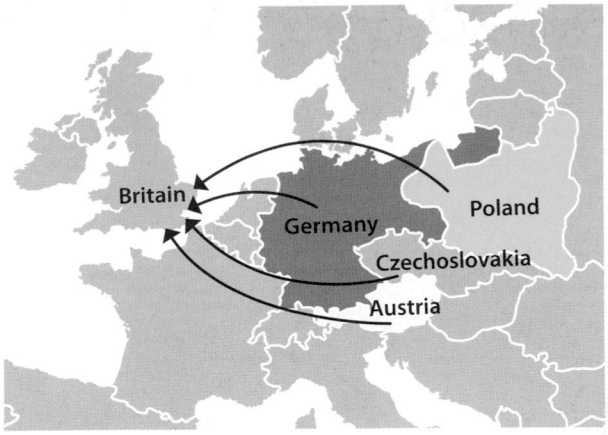

Fleeing to freedom

The map shows the long journeys made across Europe to Britain from countries where Jewish people feared for their lives.

Kindertransport refugee statue at Liverpool Street station in London

Children took their favourite toys with them.

Nicholas Winton in 1938, with one of the children he rescued.

Escape by train

Nicholas Winton was a British Jew who wanted to help Jewish people. He went to Czechoslovakia (today Czech Republic and Slovakia) and met Jewish families who wanted their children sent to safety. He found new homes for the refugees, and trains to take them there. The first train left one day before the Nazis arrived. The last left the day before Britain went to war. In total, 669 children safely reached Britain.

Evacuees

Some British children living in towns and cities left home too. Families were under threat of bomb or gas attacks, so the government said children should go to the country. More than a million evacuees packed their bags, and parents saw them off onto buses and trains.

Evacuees wore labels that showed their name, address, school, and where they were going.

War begins

When Germany attacked Poland on 1 September, 1939, France and Britain declared war on Germany two days later. By the spring of 1940, fighting had spread. Germany invaded Denmark and Norway. Then it attacked the Netherlands, Belgium, and France. The German army was in control.

Poland invaded, September, 1939

Hitler saluted his soldiers as they left to invade Poland. British reporter Clare Hollingworth was in Poland at the time. She heard guns in the night and phoned the British embassy to say war had begun.

British army gas mask

WOW!

Every person in Britain had a **gas mask.** That's a total of **38 million masks!**

Preparing for air raids, September, 1939

People in Britain got ready for air raids. They hung blackout curtains at the windows to stop enemy pilots seeing lights at night. Each person had a gas mask, in case poison gas bombs fell.

This map shows German advances up to the summer of 1940.

Dutch cities bombed, May, 1940

After Rotterdam in the Netherlands was bombed, the Dutch government surrendered. Germany used a new way of fighting called *blitzkrieg*, meaning "lightning war". They sent in bombers and tanks to create terror before ground troops arrived.

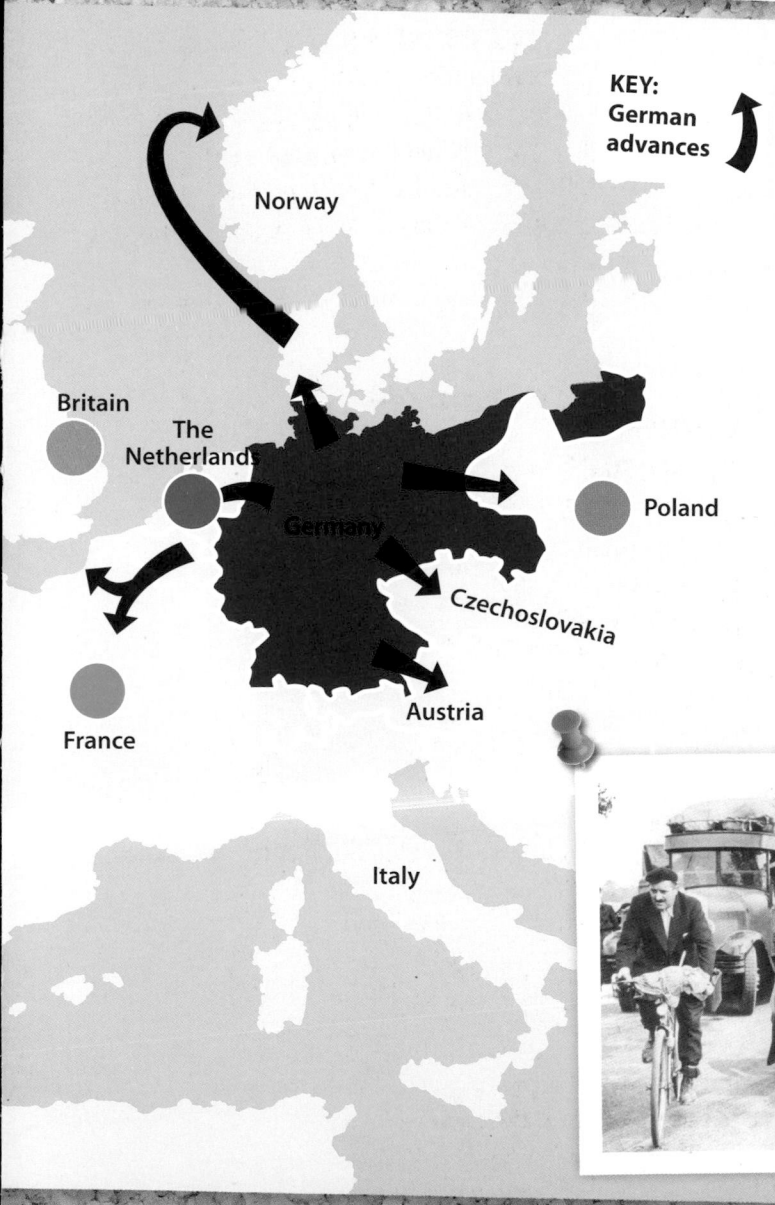

Norway invaded, June, 1940

German troops took over Denmark, then Norway. Britain and France sent help, but Norway had to surrender in June, 1940. German troops were in control.

Fall of France, June, 1940

Germany invaded France in May, 1940. Refugees (people escaping war) took all they could carry as they tried to get away. On 22 June, 1940, France surrendered to Germany.

Key players

About 50 countries joined the war, as fighting spread from Europe to Asia and the Pacific Ocean. Some countries joined the Axis (with Germany). Others chose the Allies (with Britain, France, the USA, and the Soviet Union).

The Axis

Nazi Germany, with Adolf Hitler as leader, led the Axis side. Germany's main ally (partner) in Europe was Italy. Japan joined the Axis later in 1941, when it attacked the USA.

GERMANY

Leader: ADOLF HITLER

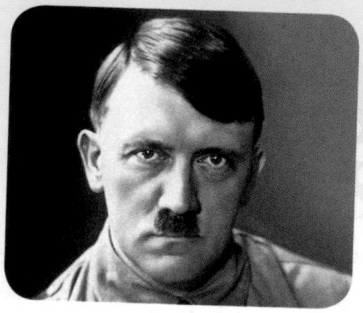

Adolf Hitler (1889–1945) led Nazi Germany from 1933. He wanted revenge for losing World War I (1914–18). He held huge rallies and tried to turn people against Jews and Communists. He killed himself a week before Germany surrendered.

JAPAN

Leader: EMPEROR HIROHITO

Hirohito (1901–89) became Japan's emperor in 1926. He was against Japan's war plans in the 1930s, but agreed to attack Pearl Harbor, USA, in 1941. In 1945 he took part in Japan's surrender, and told his people to stop treating him as a god.

ITALY

Leader: BENITO MUSSOLINI

Benito Mussolini (1883–1945) led Fascist Italy from 1922. He wanted Italy to be a modern Roman Empire, and so became Hitler's ally. In 1940, Italy joined the war, but left the Axis in 1943. Mussolini was later caught and killed just before the war ended.

The Allies

Britain and France were allies. They went to war with Germany in 1939, after Germany attacked Poland. Other nations, including Australia, New Zealand, and Canada, joined the Allies. In 1941, so did the Soviet Union (Russia), the USA, and China.

USA

Leader: FRANKLIN D. ROOSEVELT

Franklin D. Roosevelt (1882–1945) was US president from 1933. He helped America recover from hard times in the 1930s. The USA joined the Allies in 1941, when Japan attacked Pearl Harbor. Roosevelt died just before the war ended.

GREAT BRITAIN

Leader: WINSTON CHURCHILL

Winston Churchill (1874–1965) became Britain's prime minister in 1940 when the country was in already at war. Churchill's speeches inspired people to fight on. He worked closely with other Allied leaders, especially US President Roosevelt.

SOVIET UNION

Leader: JOSEPH STALIN

Joseph Stalin (1878–1953) ruled the Soviet Union from 1924. He got rid of all who stood in his way. Stalin had agreed with Hitler there would be no war between them, but in June 1941, Germany invaded Russia. The Russians fought back and defeated them.

! REALLY?

Britain, the USA, and the Soviet Union were called the "Big Three".

Soldiers in Paris
German soldiers occupied Paris, the French capital, from June 1940 until August 1944. This group of German soldiers are walking by the Eiffel Tower.

Living with the enemy

By 1940, Hitler's armies had moved into much of Europe. People in Poland, Norway, the Netherlands, and most of France lived under German occupation. This meant they lived under enemy rule. People had to do what the Germans told them. Not everyone followed their rules, and some fought back in secret.

Fighting back

Secret groups of fighters called the French Resistance tried to stop Nazi rule. The Allies dropped weapons for them by parachute. They also sent in secret agents to help.

Secret messages
Resistance fighters sent secret messages using Morse code. Tapping keys on machines like this sent coded information by radio.

Resistance fighters in Paris, 1944, helping overthrow German rule.

Street fighters
Men and women joined the Resistance. Some fought battles in the streets of towns and villages.

WOW!

Lysander planes flew **secret agents** in and out of France. They often landed in fields.

French hero
Jean Moulin (1899–1943) played a very important part in the Resistance. He used the code name Max. Moulin escaped to Britain, but returned to France to help lead the Resistance. He was killed in 1943.

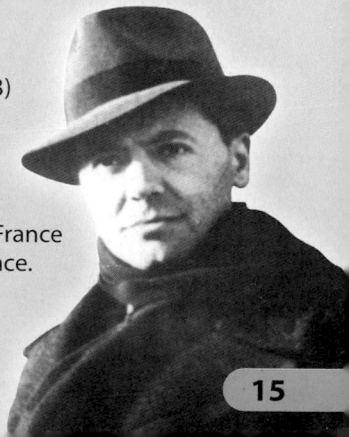

Operation Dynamo

German armies invaded France in May, 1940, pushing Allied soldiers out. Many gathered at a port on the north coast of France called Dunkirk. The Germans closed in, trapping thousands of British and French men on the beaches. It seemed hopeless, but the Allies launched a mission called Operation Dynamo.

Pushed back to the English Channel, British and French troops faced defeat. Surprisingly, Hitler ordered the Germans to stop. This gave the Allies valuable time to plan an escape for the stranded men.

The men at Dunkirk were out in the open, with nowhere to hide. They had to dig into the sand for shelter from German dive-bombers. Many soldiers were injured as the battle raged for days.

Britain sent all the ships it could, even small fishing boats. These "little ships", as they were called, sailed into shore to rescue the men.

Soldiers waded out to the rescue boats. Big ships carried more men, but had to wait further from shore than the smaller craft.

Troops were forced to leave their heavy guns and vehicles behind. Most had only rifles as they crowded onto the boats. German bombs and torpedoes made the sea-crossing back to Britain very dangerous.

Operation Dynamo was expected to rescue around 35,000 troops. In just nine days, 900 ships saved 338,000 British and French soldiers.

Britain's Prime Minister Churchill called the rescue "a miracle".

The Dunkirk Medal was given to the soldiers at Dunkirk.

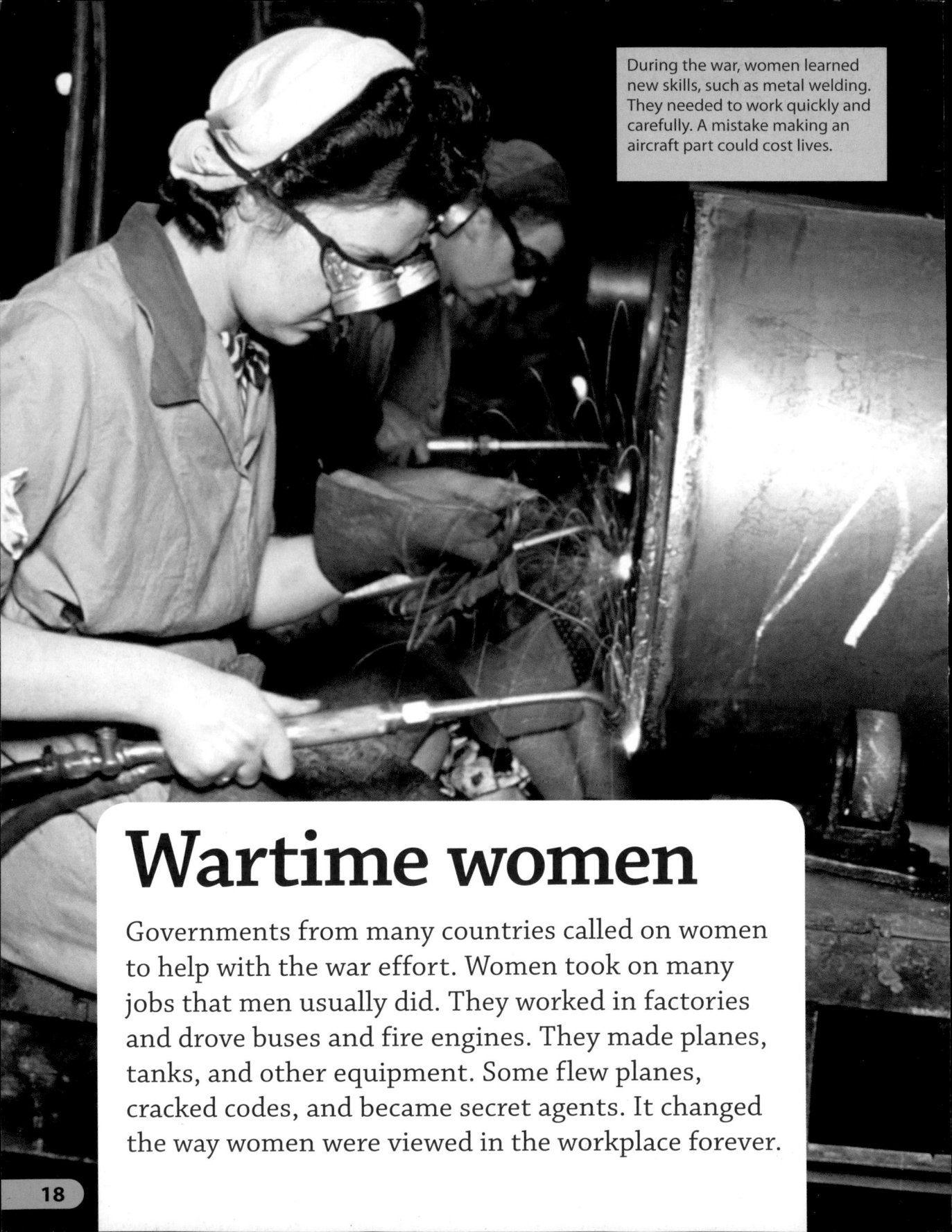

During the war, women learned new skills, such as metal welding. They needed to work quickly and carefully. A mistake making an aircraft part could cost lives.

Wartime women

Governments from many countries called on women to help with the war effort. Women took on many jobs that men usually did. They worked in factories and drove buses and fire engines. They made planes, tanks, and other equipment. Some flew planes, cracked codes, and became secret agents. It changed the way women were viewed in the workplace forever.

Lettice Curtis

Expert pilot Lettice Curtis flew fighter and bomber planes. Along with other British women, she took new planes to air bases. Women pilots in the USA and Australia did the same jobs.

Land Army

To grow more food, people planted vegetables in parks and gardens. Women in Britain and the USA joined the Land Army to work on farms.

Posters, like this one from the USA, showed how women could help the war effort.

Women pilots of the Night Bomber Regiment.

Soviet pilots

In the Soviet Union (Russia), women also fought in the war. This photograph shows a group of female pilots. Nicknamed *Nachthexen* (Night Witches) by the Nazis, these pilots dropped bombs in the dark. They switched off the engine and glided to the target. The enemy did not hear them coming, until the bombs fell.

Luftwaffe

The German air force, or *Luftwaffe*, sent 1,500 aircraft into battle. They flew from airfields in France and Norway. German pilots had fought air battles before. They were confident that they would win.

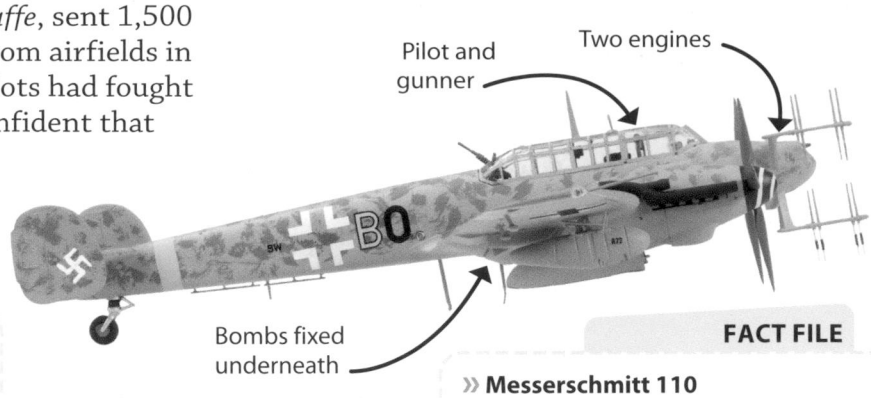

FACT FILE

» **Heinkel III**
This German bomber's job was to bomb RAF airfields.

» **Crew:** five

» **Speed:** 400 kph (255 mph)

FACT FILE

» **Messerschmitt 110**
This German fighter had seven guns. Its job was to protect the bombers.

» **Crew:** two

» **Speed:** 560 kph (349 mph)

18 June — British prime minister Winston Churchill tells parliament, "The Battle of Britain is about to begin".

10 July — Air battles begin after *Luftwaffe* planes bomb British ships in the English Channel.

27 July — *Luftwaffe* planes flew across the Channel to attack Britain.

12 August — RAF fights off German attacks on airfields and radar stations in England.

13 August — German use codename *Adlertag* ("Eagle Day") for mass attack. Hundreds of planes battle over southern England.

Battle of Britain

Hitler planned to invade Britain in June, 1940. He knew he would have to destroy Britain's Royal Air Force (RAF) first. Only then could the German army cross the English Channel, safe from air attack. The fierce fighting between the German and British air forces was called the Battle of Britain.

Royal Air Force

Britain's RAF began the battle with about 500 fighter aircraft. Many pilots were young, but they learned quickly. Britain also had radar. Radar used sound waves to pick out enemy planes and show where they were.

FACT FILE

» **Spitfire**
This was the fastest British fighter. It had eight guns to shoot down enemy planes.

» **Crew:** one

» **Speed:** 570 kph (355 mph)

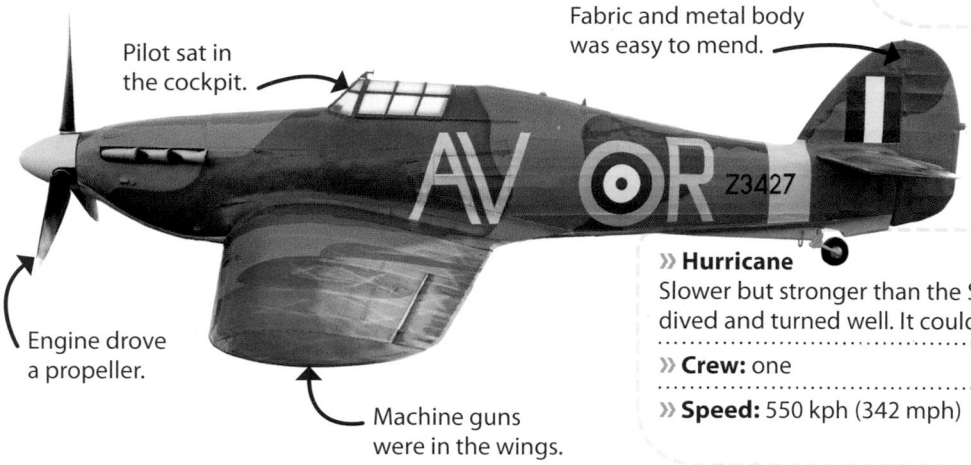

FACT FILE

» **Hurricane**
Slower but stronger than the Spitfire, the Hurricane dived and turned well. It could chase German bombers.

» **Crew:** one

» **Speed:** 550 kph (342 mph)

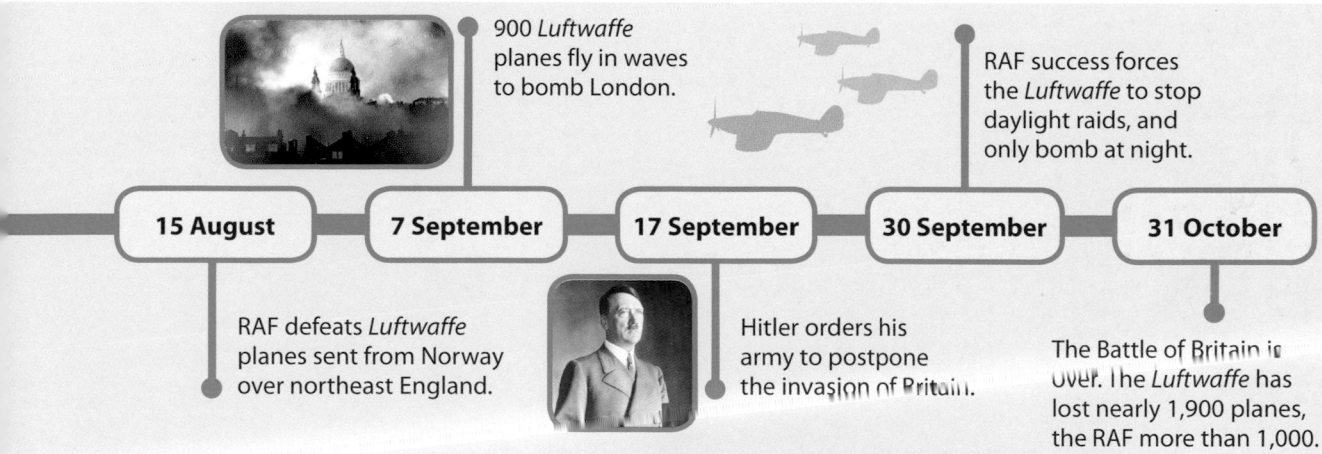

Who won?

Throughout the summer of 1940, people on the ground watched battles in the sky, called dogfights. Bombs fell and planes crashed, but Hitler's army did not invade Britain. He told the *Luftwaffe* to bomb cities instead. The RAF had won the Battle of Britain. However, the war was not over yet.

This German Heinkel III was shot down and crashed in Essex.

Propaganda

Countries didn't only use weapons to fight the war. Propaganda is the use of words and pictures to get people to think in a certain way. Governments on both sides used propaganda to make people do things for their country. They tried to make the enemy look bad and keep their side thinking they could win, sometimes by lying to people with news that was false.

This poster from the USA shows a female factory worker. It was used to get people to "roll up their sleeves" and work hard.

This Nazi poster urges French people to switch sides and join them. "You will win", the poster promises.

Posters

Bold posters were used for many purposes by both sides. People were encouraged to work hard, look out for spies, and waste nothing. Posters were displayed at school, work, and in the street.

American soldiers listening to news from back home.

Radio

In the days before television, people got a lot of their news from the radio. War leaders used radio to give rousing speeches. The enemy tried to spread fear with fake news, but it often seemed far-fetched and not believable.

Cartoons like this made fun of the enemy.

Newspapers

Governments told newspapers what to print, to make sure no war secrets slipped out. When battles were won, the headlines and stories were big. When battles were lost, they were much smaller. Adverts gave tips on keeping fit and safe.

German director Leni Riefenstahl made films of Nazi rallies and the Berlin Olympics.

Film

People loved going to the cinema. Before a film, newsreels (short films) showed victories in battle and people working hard for the war effort. Many films had war themes.

WOW!

Allied planes dropped **6 billion propaganda leaflets** on Europe.

War savings

The war cost huge sums of money. Government posters asked people to buy War Bonds. This was a way of helping the war effort and saving money at the same time.

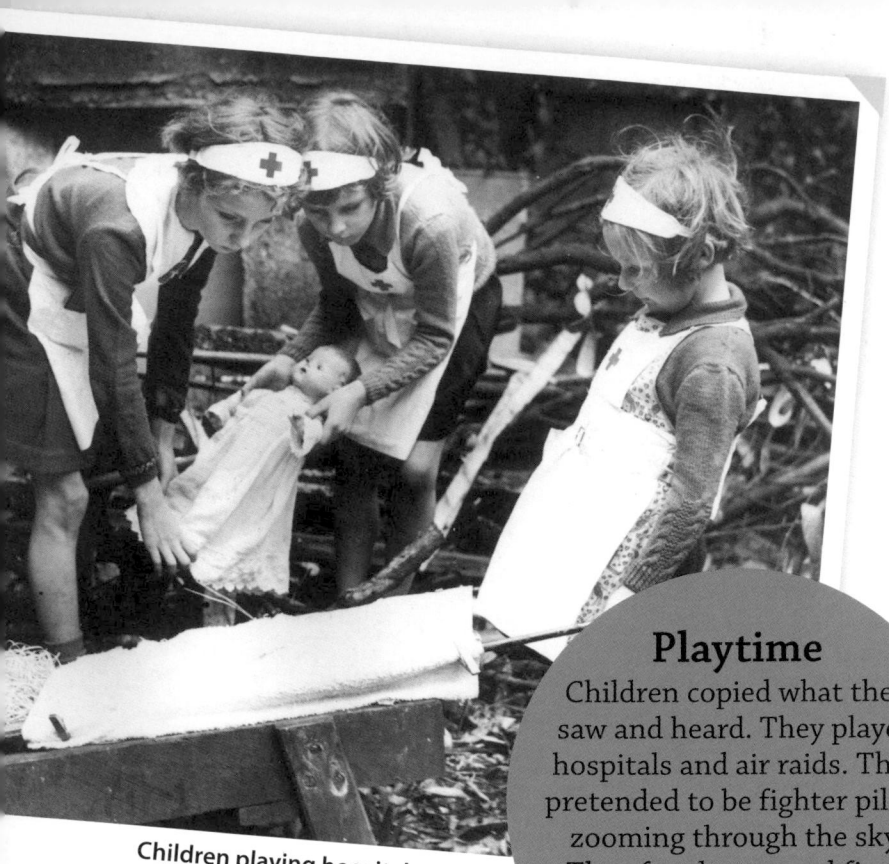

Children playing hospitals with their dolls.

Toys

Children played with old, patched-up dolls, teddies, and bikes. Many toys had war themes. Most toys were made of wood. Metal and plastic were valuable, and so rarer.

Playtime

Children copied what they saw and heard. They played hospitals and air raids. They pretended to be fighter pilots zooming through the sky. They fought pretend fires, drove ambulances, or marched like soldiers.

Wartime entertainment

People all over the world had a lot to worry about in wartime. They needed cheering up, and entertainers did their bit for the war effort. Radio, films, music, and sport all helped people to carry on. Children still played games, but new toys were a real treat.

Casablanca (1942), a wartime love story

Movies

People went to the cinema to escape the worries of war and be entertained. They enjoyed romantic dramas, such as the US film *Casablanca*.

Games

Many board games and playing cards had wartime themes. Some featured new characters, such as warden and evacuee. Battle puzzles and "hunt-the-sub" games were also popular.

Evacuee card game was a wartime version of "Happy Families".

Homemade wooden truck and plane

Radio

Families gathered around the radio (called a "wireless") to listen to the news. They enjoyed comedy, variety shows, and music. There were radio shows for children too, with stories, talks, and songs.

Entertaining the troops

Stars gave live shows for troops and factory workers. British singer Vera Lynn was famous for her wartime songs. *Lili Marlene* was a well-known song that was popular with both Allied and Axis audiences.

Vera Lynn singing to British troops in 1940.

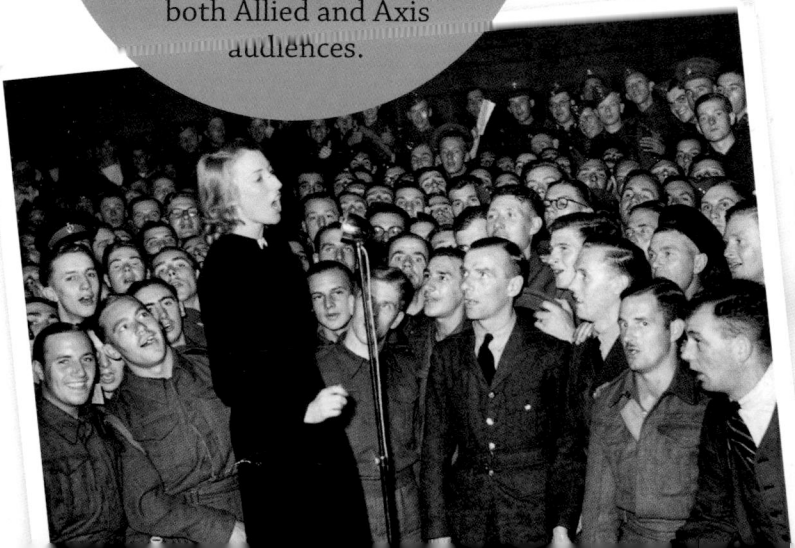

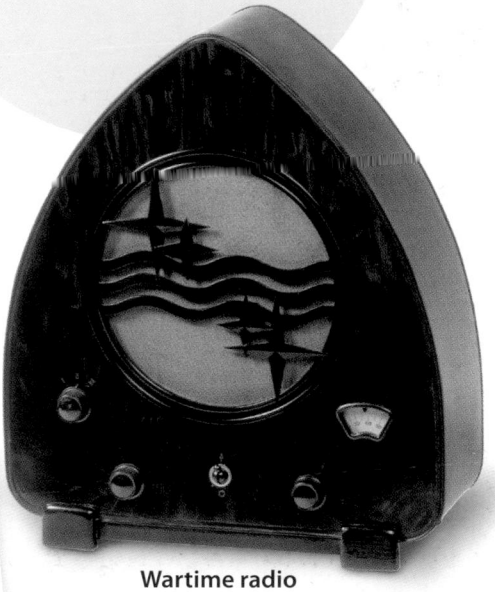

Wartime radio

Battles at sea

Naval forces fought battles at sea, above and below the waves. Cargo ships travelled in groups (convoys) with food, oil, and other supplies. Warships cruised on the surface. Submarines moved beneath the waves, while aircraft flew overhead.

Acanthus

Small warships protected cargo ships and hunted submarines. They cleared away floating bombs, called mines. *Acanthus*, built in Britain, fought in Norway's navy.

Bismarck had eight big guns and 44 smaller guns. It also had two aircraft.

Hornet

The US Navy's *Hornet* was an aircraft carrier, with 90 planes. It sank in 1942, in a battle in the Pacific Ocean.

Planes took off from the flat deck, or carrier. They landed on it, too.

Japanese I-400

This was the war's biggest submarine, at 122 m (400 ft) long. It had a crew of 144 and could carry aircraft, even underwater!

The submarine had to surface before a plane took off. A catapult sent the plane into the air to spy over the sea.

Liberator

The US Liberator bombers flew far out over the Atlantic Ocean. They were used to hunt German submarines. When Liberators found a submarine, they attacked it with bombs.

Wings and engines were high up, to keep clear of the water.

Sunderland

These British flying boats could take off and land on water. Each had a crew of 10, with eight guns, as well as bombs. They could fly 4,000 km (2,485 miles).

Condor

German pilots flew Condors on sea patrols. They hunted Allied ships, dropping bombs to sink them. Condors could fly non-stop for up to 14 hours.

Bismarck

The mighty *Bismarck* was one of the German navy's greatest battleships. British warships chased and sank it in 1941.

German U-boat

Short for "undersea boats", U-boats were German submarines. They lay hidden underwater, ready to fire missiles at ships. Submarines used electric motors underwater and diesel motors on the surface.

The captain could look around using a periscope, while the U-boat was hidden beneath the surface.

GI Joe the pigeon

Trained pigeons carried messages tied to their legs. GI Joe once saved 100 Allied soldiers from being bombed by their own side by flying 32 km (20 miles) in 20 minutes. This gave the soldiers time to get away.

Upstart the police horse

Upstart worked in London during air raids. Once, a bomb exploded nearby, and he was lucky to survive. Glass and metal flew through the air, but Upstart stayed calm. He led people to safety while more bombs fell.

Animal heroes

Did you know that animals went to war, too? Some even won medals, such as the Dickin Medal, for bravery. The first winners of this medal were three pigeons, in 1943. They delivered urgent messages that saved many lives. Other animal heroes included dogs and horses. To be awarded a Dickin Medal took special courage.

The PDSA Dickin Medal

Rex the mine dog

Rex was a stray black labrador. Working with the British Army, like the dog pictured, his keen nose sniffed out land mines. Mines were small bombs, hidden just under the ground. Brave Rex saved many soldiers.

A ship's cat

Many ships kept a cat to keep disease-carrying rats away. Cats at sea lived through battles, storms, and even shipwrecks. When danger was over, most cats found a warm place to curl up and go to sleep.

5 ANIMAL HERO FACTS

1. **Judy the pointer dog** comforted people who were locked up in Japanese prison camps.
2. **Rip the stray dog** helped to find people hurt during the air raids on London in 1941.
3. **Sheila the collie dog** rescued four US airmen lost in the snow after a plane crash in Scotland.
4. **Regal the police horse** kept calm when his London stable was fire-bombed – twice.
5. **Rifleman Khan the German shepherd dog** saved a soldier from drowning during a battle in the Netherlands.

Tanks into Russia

In June 1941, German armies marched into Russia, which was then part of the Soviet Union. Hitler had broken his word not to attack the country. He sent 3 million men and 3,000 tanks into Russia, hoping for a quick victory. But Russia is a huge country and its winters are freezing cold. The invasion turned into the most terrible battle of the war so far. The fighting in Russia lasted for four years, until early 1945.

German PzKW III

Fast-moving German tanks travelled in groups. Each tank had a crew of five. It had a commander, a driver, a radio man, and two gunners. The commander gave orders by radio.

Battle for Stalingrad

In 1942, the Russian city of Stalingrad became a battlefield. When the winter came, the German army froze. Soldiers had little warm clothing, food, or fuel. Russian fighters trapped 250,000 Germans in the city. They surrendered in January, 1943. In total, the battle cost more than one million lives on both sides, including Russian civilians.

Street fighting
This photo shows Russian troops fighting back in Stalingrad. They were better prepared for the freezing conditions.

A revolving turret could swing the gun right round.

The commander had the best view from the domed top, or cupola.

The main gun was powerful enough to blast holes in buildings.

The smaller machine gun was next to the tank's driver.

German stick grenade
After pulling a cord, German soldiers had only a few seconds to throw one of these bombs before it exploded.

Straw boots
Some German soldiers wore straw boots over their ordinary boots. They were trying to keep their feet warm and dry in the snow.

Harsh winters
People in Stalingrad suffered cold and hunger. Many died on both sides. The city lay in ruins.

Air power

During World War II, people in factories worked hard to make bombers, fighters, and transport planes. New aircraft were bigger, better, and faster than ever before. The Allies' mighty air power helped them to win the war.

WOW!

Only a Lancaster could carry a Grand Slam bomb, which was as heavy as two elephants!

Avro Lancaster

The Lancaster was the RAF's best bomber. Hundreds flew from Britain to bomb targets in Germany at night. The Lancaster had the same engine as the Spitfire.

FACT FILE

» **Speed:** 438 kph (272 mph)

» **Crew:** seven

» **Weapons:** eight machine guns in three turrets and 6,350 kg (14,000 lbs) of bombs

De Havilland Mosquito

Unusually, Mosquitoes were made mostly of wood. They were very fast fighters or bombers. Mosquitoes also flew in front of Lancasters, dropping flares to light up targets.

FACT FILE

» **Speed:** 589 kph (366 mph)

» **Crew:** two

» **Weapons:** four cannons in nose, machine guns, bombs and cameras for taking pictures of enemy targets

Douglas C-47 Skytrain

More than 10,000 of these US transport planes were built. C-47s carried troops, supplies, and wounded soldiers. They also flew secret agents into Nazi-occupied Europe.

FACT FILE

» **Speed:** 370 kph (230 mph)

» **Crew:** three

» **Weapons:** no guns, instead carried 2,722 kg (6,000 lbs) of cargo, or 28 paratroopers, or 14 wounded soldiers

Tail fin showed the Nazi swastika

Pilot sat in the cockpit

Long nose helped make the aircraft streamlined

Two turbojet engines sucked in air, forcing it out at the rear

Messerschmitt Me262

The first jet warplane was Germany's *Sturmvogel* (Storm Bird). With no propellers, its speed took the Allies by surprise in 1944. However, jet planes came too late to save Germany.

FACT FILE

» **Speed:** 870 kph (540 mph)

» **Crew:** one

» **Weapons:** four guns in nose (carrying bombs slowed the jet down)

P-51 Mustang

The Mustang was America's best fighter plane. It was fast and could also fly far. Mustangs flew from Britain to Germany, to defend Allied bombers from enemy fighters.

FACT FILE

» **Speed:** 703 kph (437 mph)

» **Crew:** one

» **Weapons:** six machine guns, plus rockets and bombs for attacking tanks, trains, and trucks

Kawasaki Ki-100

Japan's Ki-100 could fly very high, reaching heights of more than 10,000 m (33,000 ft). It was rushed into action in 1945 to fight high-flying Allied bombers.

FACT FILE

» **Speed:** 590 kph (367 mph)

» **Crew:** one

» **Weapons:** four guns in fuselage (body) and wings, plus bombs or extra fuel tanks

The Holocaust

Hitler and the Nazis forced Jewish people to live in Jewish-only areas, called ghettos. The ghettos were shut off from outside help, and conditions were unbearable. People were also sent to camps. Over six million Jewish people and other groups of people who Hitler thought of as "undesirable" were killed. After the war, in 1945, the world learned of the Nazis' mass murders, called the Holocaust.

Yellow star

Nazis made Jewish people wear a yellow star on their clothes in the ghettos and in the camps. On it was the word *Jude* (Jew). Every camp prisoner had a number tattooed on their arm.

Auschwitz

The camps that the Nazis sent people to were called concentration camps. The biggest one was Auschwitz, in Poland. The Nazis killed more than one million people there. Trains carried men, women, and children to the camp every day.

Concentration camps

The camps were built across Europe. Here, people were forced to work. Along with Jews were people who spoke out or fought against the Nazis. Many prisoners died from illness, hunger, and harsh treatment. Others were killed.

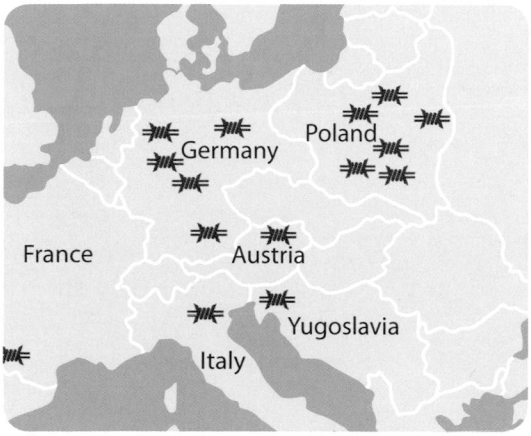

Map showing where the biggest camps were.

This is the gateway to Auschwitz. Today, people visit the site to remember the dead.

Remembering the Holocaust

Every year, Holocaust Memorial Day is held on 27 January. People remember those who died. They mark this special day in the hope that nothing like the Holocaust ever happens again.

Holocaust Memorial in Pennsylvania, USA.

Anne Frank

Anne Frank was a German Jewish girl. To escape the Nazis, her family fled to Amsterdam in the Netherlands. However, in 1940, the Nazis arrived in Amsterdam. Fearing for their lives, the family hid in two rooms behind an office wall. It was there that Anne wrote her diary.

Anne wrote her diary by hand in small notebooks. She added photographs to remind her of times gone by. In the entries below, Anne talks about her grandmother with great fondness.

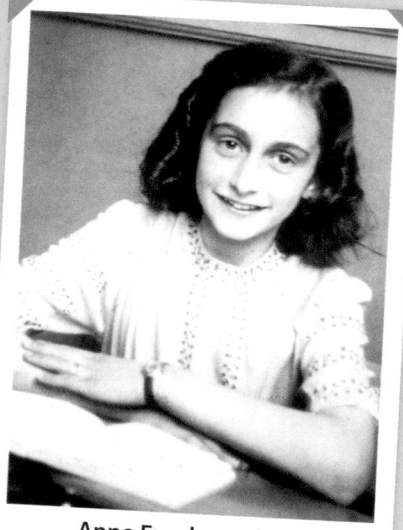

Anne Frank aged 12, before she went into hiding.

Young writer

Anne was born in 1929. She loved to write and, from her 13th birthday, kept a diary. She wrote about growing up and how it felt to be shut away, hiding from the Nazis.

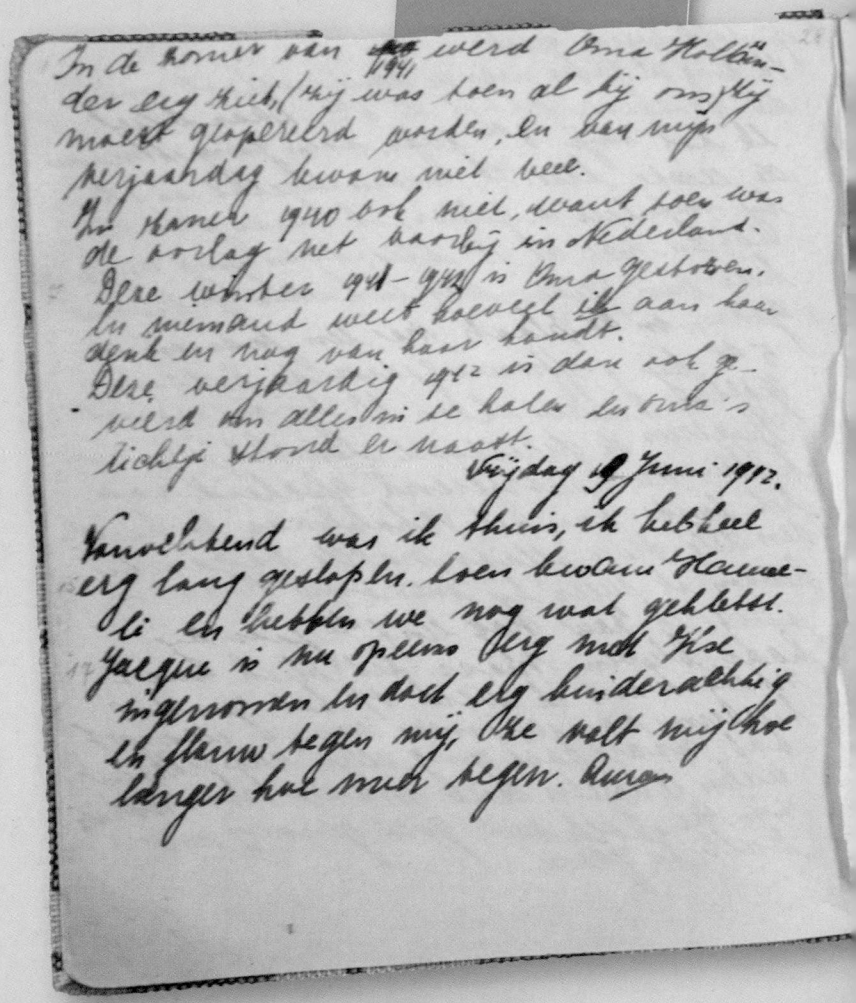

In de kamer van ~~[illegible]~~ 1941 werd Oma Holländer erg ziek, zij was toen al bij mijn moeder gepensioneerd worden, en kon mijn verjaardag kwam niet meer.
Het kamer 1940 ook niet, want toen was de oorlog net begonnen in Nederland.
Deze winter 1941-1942 is Oma gestorben, en niemand weet hoeveel ik aan haar denk en nog van haar houdt.
Deze verjaardag 1942 is dan ook gepeld door alleen de kaler en onze is lichtje stond en naast.

Vrijdag 9 Juni 1942.

Vanochtend was ik thuis, ik heb heel erg lang geslapen. Toen kwam Hannelie en hebben we nog wat gekletst. Jacque is nu pleno erg met Hse ingekomen en doet erg kinderachtig en flauw tegen mij, die valt mij hoe langer hoe meer tegen. Anne

Nazi rule

Under Nazi rule, Jewish people in the Netherlands could not live normal lives. They had to wear a yellow star to single them out. They could not use public transport or ride bikes. Jewish children weren't allowed to go to school. In 1942, the Frank family feared Anne's sister Margot would be sent to a work-camp. The family hid above Mr Frank's office.

Nazi soldiers march through a Dutch town in May, 1940.

This photo shows Anne with her older sister, Margot. Her grandmother is in the background.

This photo shows Anne with Margot one year later.

Secret doorway into the Frank family's hiding place.

The secret hideout

Four people joined the Frank family in their two-room hiding place. One was an older boy, Peter, who became a friend. They could not go out, but friends brought food and news. Anne was in hiding from 1942 to 1944. Then Nazi police came and took them away. Anne died in Bergen-Belsen camp, in 1945. She was 16 years old. Only her father survived the war.

Desert warfare

In 1940, war spread to North Africa. German and Italian armies faced British and Allied troops in the desert. With tanks, planes, and trucks, they fought in the heat and dust. The Allies' victory at El Alamein, Egypt, was a turning point in the war.

WOW!

Pilots kept notes written in Arabic, asking for help if they crashed in the desert.

Pilots flew over the pyramids of Egypt. They watched for enemy tanks and trucks crossing the vast North African desert.

The Desert Rats

British soldiers called themselves the Desert Rats. The little animal on their flag is a jerboa, a rodent that lives in the desert.

Desert life

In the desert, daytime temperatures soared to more than 30°C (86°F), but nights turned cold. Soldiers wore hats to protect them from the sun and lightweight clothes, including shorts. Men slept in tents or trucks. Out on patrol, they carried extra water and petrol in cans. Even tinned food melted.

Desert cap
This German Afrika Korps cap had a flap to protect the neck from sunburn. Other hats had wide brims.

Arab headdress
Some Allied soldiers took to wearing local clothes that suited desert conditions. This Arab headdress kept a soldier's head cool by day. It gave extra warmth at night.

Water bottle
Every soldier needed a canteen, or water bottle. The desert had few oases (natural wells). If a soldier ran out of water he could die.

Growing up in the war

War changed children's lives, too. Fathers left home and went to fight. Mothers went out to work. Children wondered if life would ever be the same again. Rationing meant less food to eat. There were safety drills at school. During air raids, children slept in cold, damp shelters. Even once they had grown up, people who were children in wartime never forgot the hardship and danger they faced.

Gas mask
Colourful masks like this one were given to toddlers to make them more fun to wear.

Working hard

Teachers in Japan told children that they must work for their emperor. Children worked on farms, as well as in factories. Even common food, such as rice, was rationed. It was hard to work when hungry. Radio news told people Japan was winning to keep their spirits up.

Hitler Youth

In Germany, Hitler wanted children to grow up as Nazis. Schools taught Nazi ideas and children were encouraged to join Nazi youth groups. From the age of 10, boys joined the Hitler Youth. Girls belonged to the League of German Girls. Children learned to follow orders, so that they were ready to fight.

Farm work

In Britain, children were evacuated from towns and cities to keep them safe from bombs. They went to live in the countryside and many worked on farms. They learned to milk cows and grow vegetables. Enemy prisoners of war were also sent to work on farms. Children often made friends with them.

Collecting junk

During the war, it was important not to waste anything. Americans were asked to collect junk, and children helped with this. They saved toothpaste tubes for metal, and rubber bands for tyres. Old stockings could be recycled to make parachutes for the war.

Making weapons
Weapons factories had fewer men, so women and children worked there. Children did factory work after school, making parts for planes and guns.

Uniforms
The Nazis gave German children uniforms, like soldiers. Children marched in bands, camped, and kept fit. Most joined the youth groups. It was safer to be like everybody else.

Dig for Victory
Food was in short supply. Children dug "Victory Gardens" at school, home, and in public parks. They grew vegetables, fruit, and herbs. Others, like in this photograph, would help with the harvest.

Anything goes
American children hunted for scrap metal, such as old stoves, like the boys in this picture, and tin cans. The metal was melted down and used again to make tanks, ships, and planes.

Pearl Harbor

On 7 December, 1941, hundreds of Japanese planes flew over Pearl Harbor, the US navy base in Hawaii. With no warning, the planes attacked the US navy base, which held almost 100 warships. They left ships on fire or sinking. It angered Americans and pushed them to join the war.

Pearl Harbor on fire
Ships were blown up and many sank. Hundreds onboard died. Rescuers fought to put out fires and save lives.

3 PEARL HARBOR FACTS

1. **The 360 Japanese planes** hit all eight battleships in port. Later, six ships went back into action.
2. **More than 2,000 people** were killed in the attack. More than 1,000 were hurt.
3. **Japan had 33 ships** north of Hawaii. Their pilots flew from six aircraft carriers. They lost 29 planes in the attack.

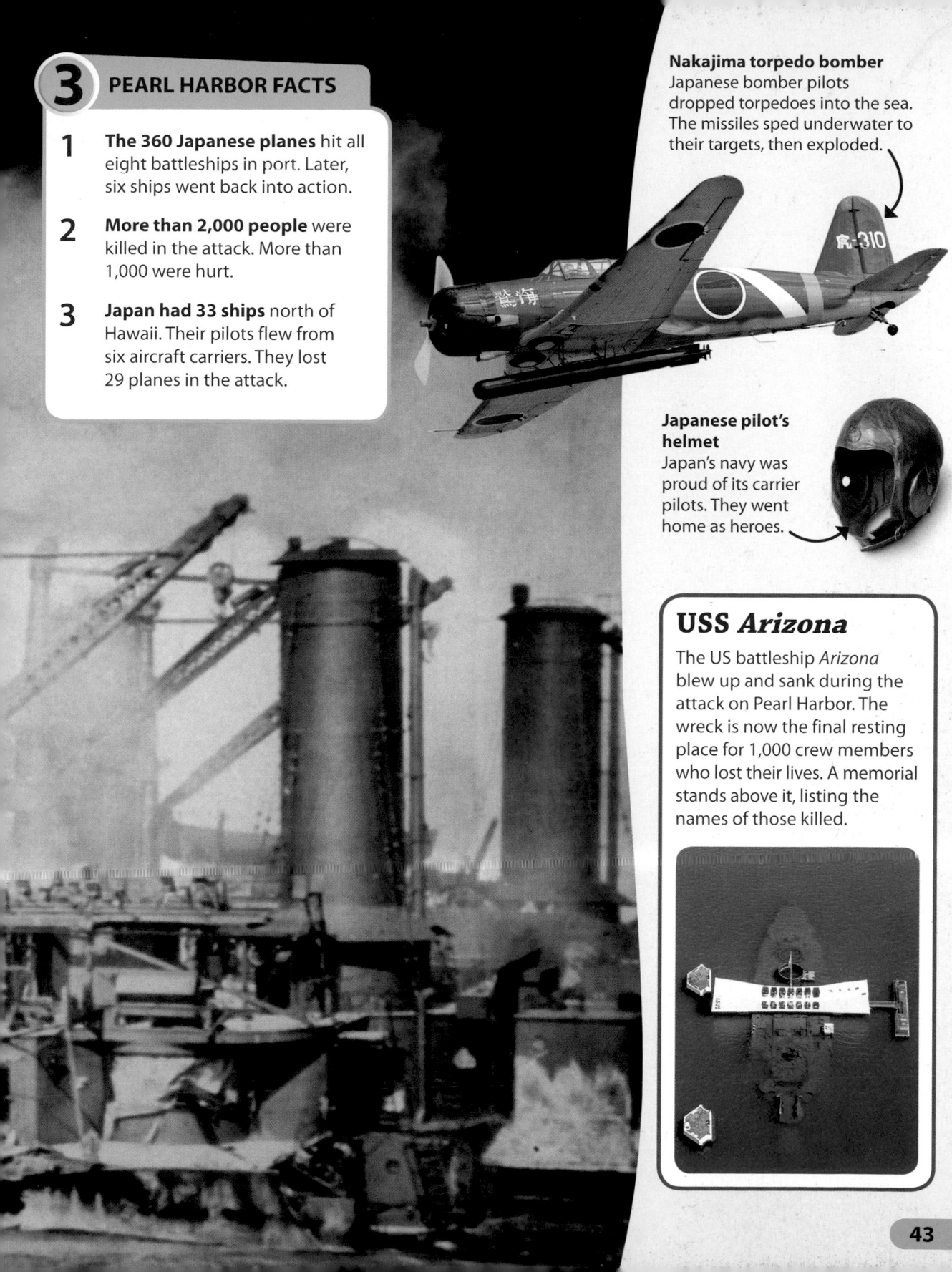

Nakajima torpedo bomber
Japanese bomber pilots dropped torpedoes into the sea. The missiles sped underwater to their targets, then exploded.

Japanese pilot's helmet
Japan's navy was proud of its carrier pilots. They went home as heroes.

USS *Arizona*

The US battleship *Arizona* blew up and sank during the attack on Pearl Harbor. The wreck is now the final resting place for 1,000 crew members who lost their lives. A memorial stands above it, listing the names of those killed.

Weekly rations

Everywhere food was rationed. Even babies had a ration book. Children got more milk and eggs than grown-ups, but less of everything else. Babies got free orange juice, too.

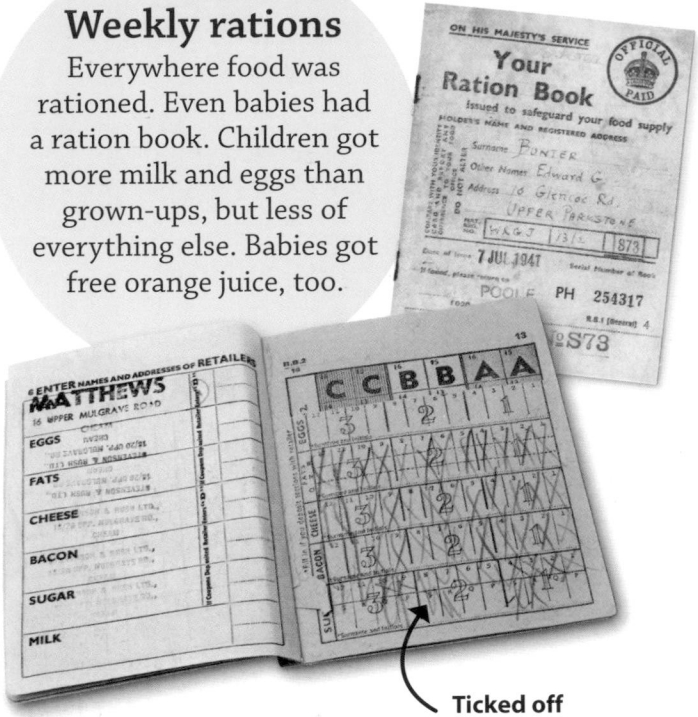

Ration book
Everyone was given a ration book to show at each shop they went to. They handed over coupons and money to buy their rations.

Ticked off
The book listed which food you could buy. Shopkeepers marked off each week's coupon.

Sugar
Many people stopped adding sugar to tea or coffee. Foods containing sugar, such as jam, cakes, and desserts, became rare treats.

Tea and coffee
Tea and coffee were rationed. US cafés had a "one-cup" coffee rule. British people might save leftover tea leaves to make the next pot.

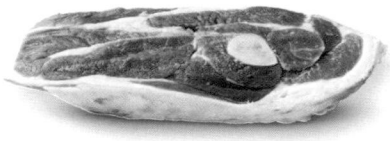

Meat
The best meat went to the army or the navy. In most countries everyone else had to make do with much less. Spam, a type of tinned meat, came over from the US in 1941 to help feed hungry Britons.

Wartime food

The war threatened food supplies. Cargo ships were now needed to carry weapons, so food from overseas vanished from shops. Fighting destroyed farms and food stores. Farmers worked harder, and governments in many countries brought in rationing. This limited how much food people could buy, giving everyone a fair share.

Bread
In Germany from the end of 1942, people were allowed only half a loaf of bread a day. Germans ate black rye bread, often mixed with "wood flour" (sawdust).

Grow your own
Vegetables were also hard to get hold off, so more people grew their own vegetables in the garden. Flowerbeds in parks were dug up and used to grow potatoes and cabbages.

Dig for Victory
This poster urged everyone to grow their own vegetables.

Milk
Milk was rationed, and people used tinned or powdered milk when they ran short.

Eggs
The shop ration in Britain was one egg a week, so many people kept hens for eggs. The US sent tins of dried eggs to Europe. Dried eggs kept for months. They were used in baking, or to make omelettes.

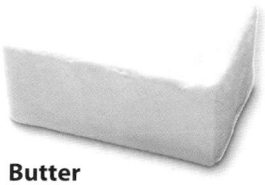

Butter
A pack of butter had to last two weeks in both Britain and Germany. Leftover fats could be collected, and turned into explosives.

Rice
In Japan, evacuee children from towns had to work in rice fields. Still, many families went hungry. In India, there was a terrible famine in 1943 when rice stocks ran out.

7 WAR FOOD FACTS

Food and drink

1. **Carrolade** was a drink made from carrot and swede juice. People also made carrot jam.
2. **In Japan**, dinner might be a fish and two vegetable leaves.
3. **In Britain,** sweets were rationed from 1942 until 1953, long after the war had ended.
4. **Germans** drank fake coffee made from acorns. Americans drank coffee with chicory and other foods added.
5. **By 1944,** many Dutch people were starving. Some people were so hungry they ate tulip bulbs.
6. **The Tower of London's** moat was dug up and used for a vegetable garden.
7. **Snoek,** a type of fish from South Africa, was shipped over to Britain in tins, because local fish were not being caught. But people hated it! After the war, tins of snoek went on sale as cat food.

WOW!

People in Europe missed fruits grown overseas, such as bananas, which were rare.

Code-breaking

In war, both sides want to keep their plans secret. They send messages in code, using mixed-up words, letters, and numbers. To read them, people must unlock the code. Both sides used machines that could do this quickly. The Allies won because they "cracked" the Axis codes first.

Enigma

German code machines were called Enigma, meaning "a puzzle". Polish scientists found out how it worked. They made a copy and showed Britain. By 1940, the British code-breakers could understand most German secret radio messages.

German Enigma machine

! WOW!

Code-breakers' jobs were top secret. They didn't tell anyone what they were doing.

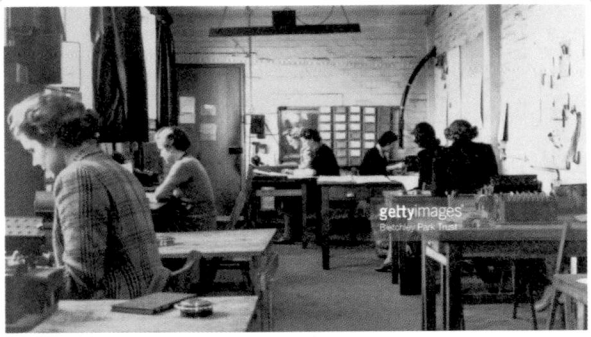

Code breakers were good at science, maths, and puzzles.

Station X

Station X was Bletchley Park, a big country house north of London. Here, more than 10,000 British code-breakers set to work. They read German radio messages and worked out codes, such as Enigma's.

Bombe

German codes changed every day. To keep up, a brilliant maths expert, along with other code-breakers at Bletchley, made a machine named the Bombe. Its spinning wheels, or rotors, could break a new code each day.

Spinning wheels
One Bombe could crack codes from 36 Enigma machines.

Colossus

The Germans also had an even better machine called Lorenz. The Bletchley code-breakers cracked it, but it was slow work, so they made the world's first electronic computer, called Colossus, to help. Colossus sorted 5,000 letters and numbers every second. Its data helped the Allies plan the D-Day landings in June, 1944.

The team at Bletchley Park built Colossus for the code-breakers.

Secret radio

Spies and agents on both sides used secret codes. They sent messages in Morse code, by radio. They often hid the radio set in a suitcase to carry around.

Suitcase spy radio

D-Day

After five years of war, Germany ruled most of Europe. The Allies were now ready to free France. They carefully planned an attack and trained troops for months. On 6 June, 1944, the Allies landed in Normandy, France. This was D-Day. By 25 August, the Allies had freed Paris from Nazi rule. Within nine months, the war in Europe was over.

Allied soldiers reached the shore in landing craft. They ran down ramps into the water and waded ashore. Other landing craft carried tanks and trucks.

3 AMAZING FACTS

Normandy invasion

1. **More than 150,000 Allied soldiers** crossed the English Channel for the attack. Around 2,500 men died in the battle.
2. **Nearly 7,000 sea craft** were used in the invasion, including battleships and minesweepers.
3. **Allied planes flew 14,000** sorties (air missions) during the attack.

Duck boat

The US DUKW was a boat with wheels. On land it became a truck. This helped allied troops land safely on D-Day.

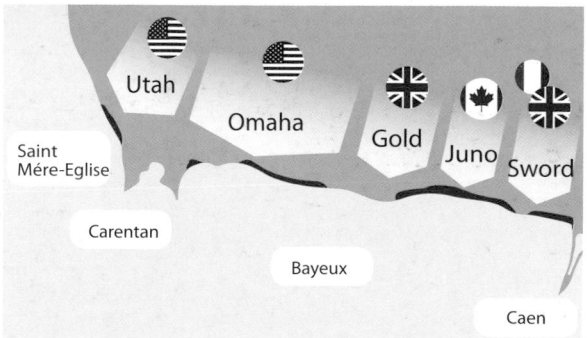

This map shows where soldiers from the USA, Britain, Canada, and France landed. Each beach had a code name.

City bombings

Air raids brought the war into people's homes. When warning sirens wailed, everyone took shelter. Bombs started fires and flattened buildings. Rescue teams helped people escape from bombed homes. Then everyone tried to repair the damage and carry on. Europe's worst city bombing happened in 1945, when Allied planes bombed the German city of Dresden.

Whistle
Hearing the warden's whistle meant "Take cover, air raid!"

Helmet
A helmet protected the warden from broken glass, metal, wood, and bricks.

Firebomb
Blazes were started with dangerous firebombs. Throwing sand or water on a firebomb could put it out.

Identity card
Everyone carried an identity card, showing the owner's name, age, address, and other details.

Air raid wardens

It was the job of air raid wardens to keep people safe during air raids. They made sure lights were out during blackouts and helped people to find shelters.

More than 1,000 Allied planes attacked Dresden. Bombs and fires destroyed its buildings. Many thousands of people died. Today, many buildings have been rebuilt, just as they were before.

War ends in Europe

After D-Day, the Allies knew they could win the war. They had more soldiers, tanks, and aircraft than Germany. In western Europe, the Americans, British, and other Allies freed France, Belgium, and the Netherlands. The Russians moved in from the east, freeing Poland. By April, 1945, they had reached Berlin. On 8 May, 1945, the war in Europe was over.

Secret weapons

Germany had secret weapons, such as V-1s, which were flying bombs. V-2s, like this one, were supersonic rockets. They came too late to change the war.

This map shows how the Allies attacked from 1943 to 1945, moving towards Germany.

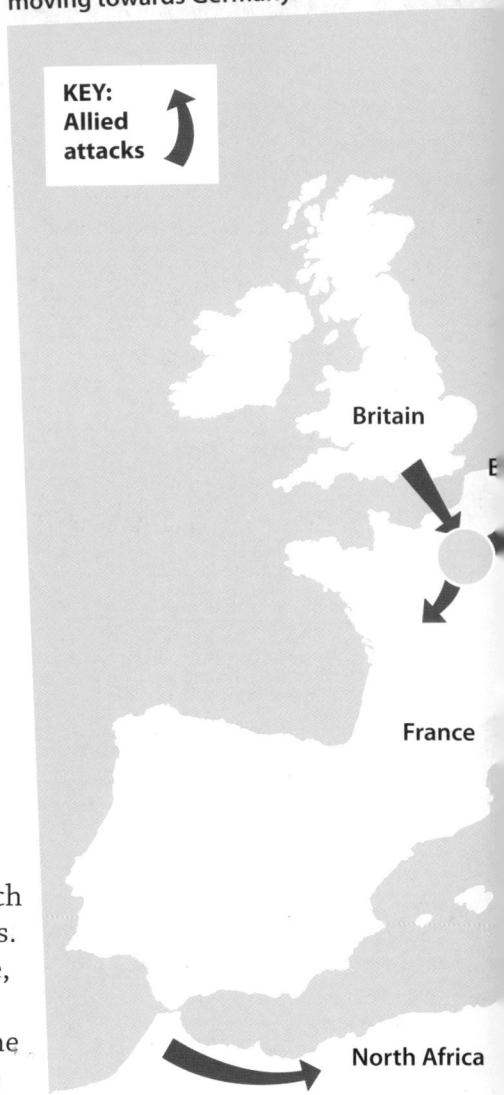

The French celebrate their freedom in 1944

Paris free

French troops fought alongside the Allied army. On 25 August, 1944, crowds cheered as French troops drove into Paris. The Germans had left. Soon afterwards, all of France was free.

Battle of the Bulge

Bad weather in December, 1944, stopped Allied planes flying. German soldiers attacked in Belgium. They pushed into the Allied line, making a "bulge". Then Allied bombers got back in the air. The German attack in the west fizzled out.

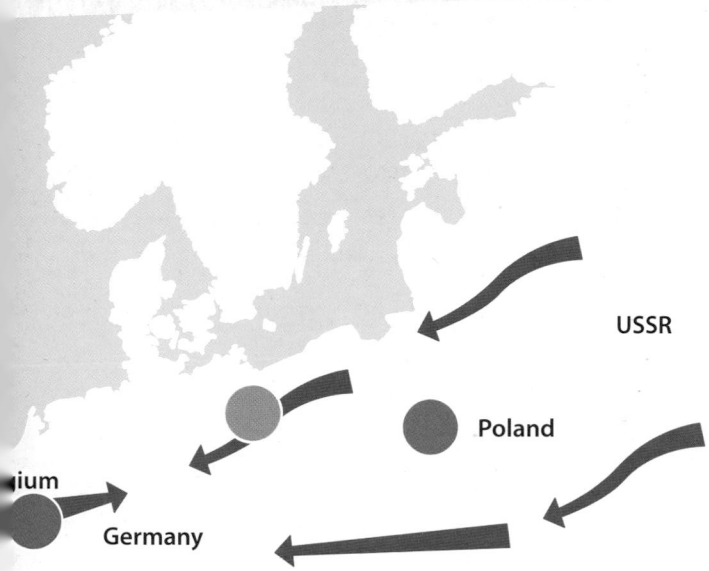

Russian Katyusha rocket launcher

Red rockets

Russia's Red Army fought across Poland and into Germany. Russian tanks, planes, and rockets destroyed German towns and villages. Many people fled west before the Red Army arrived.

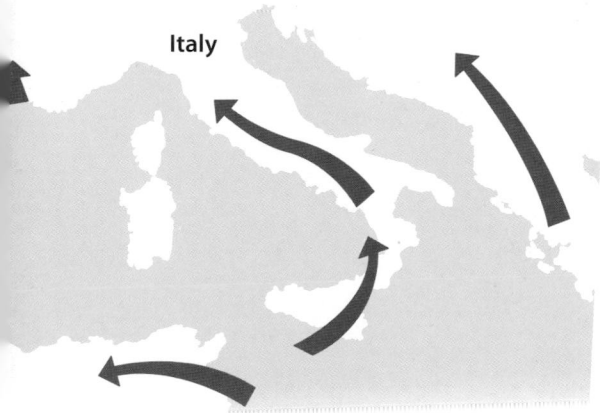

German surrender

Russians were fighting in Berlin by January, 1945. Some Nazis still hoped for peace, but others fought on. On 30 April, Hitler killed himself in his bunker (underground base). The German army surrendered days later.

EXTRA THE STARS AND STRIPES EXTRA

HITLER DEAD

Fuehrer Fell at CP, German Radio Says; Doenitz at Helm, Vows War Will Continue

Churchill Hints Peace Is at Hand

US tank in the Battle of the Bulge

VE Day

People celebrated Victory in Europe Day (VE Day) on 8 May, 1945. They danced, sang, and cheered. People waved flags, and held street parties. They also remembered. Six long years of war had left many homeless, hurt, or dead.

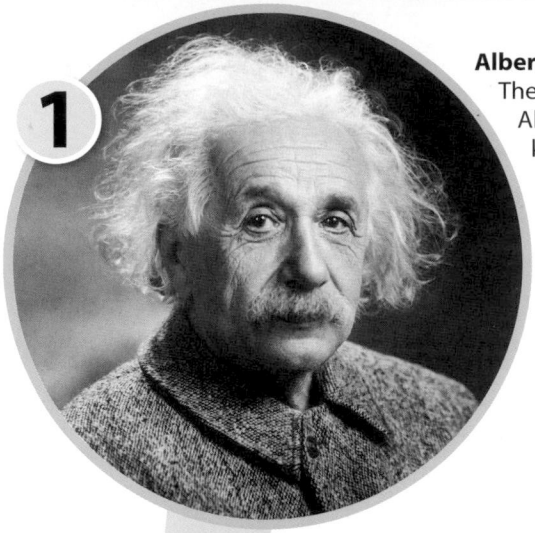

1

Albert Einstein
The great German scientist Albert Einstein (1879–1955) knew the power of atomic energy. In 1939, he warned about the terrifying threat of the atom bomb. If the Nazis made it first, the Allies would lose the war.

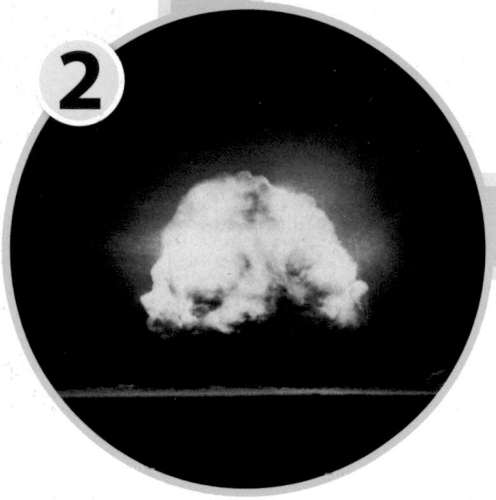

2

Manhattan Project
Allied scientists worked at Los Alamos, New Mexico, USA, from 1942. Nobody outside knew of the secret *Manhattan Project*. The project was to make the first atom bomb.

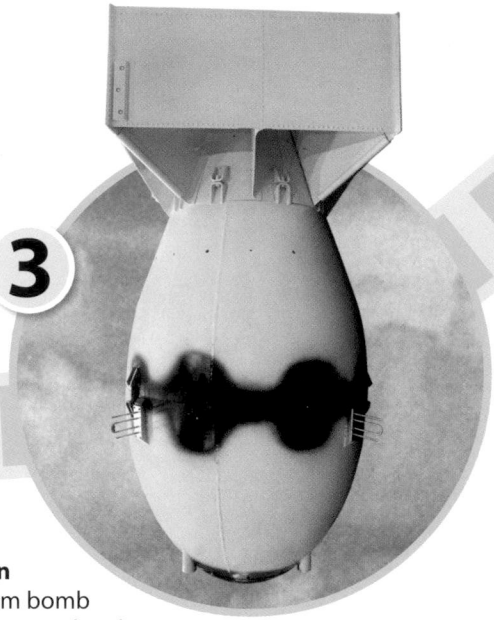

3

Fat Man
The atom bomb was first tested in the desert in New Mexico, USA, in July, 1945. The Allies made two war bombs, code-named *Little Boy* and *Fat Man*.

Atomic bomb

The Allies used a terrible new weapon in August, 1945. Just one atomic bomb was powerful enough to destroy a whole city. After two of these bombs were dropped on Japan, the fighting stopped. World War II was now over.

4

Enola Gay
On 6 August, 1945, the B-29 bomber *Enola Gay* dropped *Little Boy* on Hiroshima, Japan. Three days later, *Fat Man* exploded on Nagasaki, Japan.

5

Aftermath
The city of Hiroshima was in ruins after the atomic bomb. The city of Nagasaki was also destroyed. More than 240,000 people died because of the bombings. Japan surrendered on 15 August, 1945.

The power of atoms

Everything in the universe is made of atoms. Scientists had been working to find out how atoms produce energy. In 1942, a team in Chicago, USA, built the first atomic reactor. This machine split atoms, releasing energy. The energy could have peaceful uses, including electricity. It could also make atom bombs.

Fermi 's team
Born in Italy, Enrico Fermi was a scientist working in the USA. He led a team that showed how to control atomic power for human use.

Hiroshima today
This ruined building in Hiroshima stands as a peace memorial. It reminds people how precious peace is. It became a UNESCO World Heritage Site in 1996.

After the war

The war changed the world. The USA and the Soviet Union (Russia) were now the most powerful nations. These wartime allies soon became less friendly. Former enemies became partners. Countries which had fought the war rebuilt towns and cities. People looked towards a better and peaceful future.

Coming home

Servicemen and women looked forward to their welcome home. People were also sad, remembering friends and family they had lost in the war.

School's back

Children sent to the country for their safety came home. Work began to rebuild schools damaged by bombing. Children helped put classrooms back in order. Normal work and play began again.

Rebuilding

In Britain, one home in every three was damaged. People needed new places to live, but rebuilding took time. Factories made pre-fabricated homes that could be built quickly and were put together like furniture.

War crimes

The Allies put Nazi war leaders on trial for war crimes. The trials were held in Nuremberg, Germany. Leaders in Japan also faced punishment for their actions.

The Berlin Wall

The war ended with Germany and its capital Berlin split into two. From 1961, a wall divided the city. When the wall fell in 1989, Germany became one nation again.

The Cold War

After the war, some of the Allies became rivals. The Soviet Union (Russia) became locked in a power struggle with the USA and other Western countries. Each side wanted to show it had the best weapons. The Cold War, as it became known, lasted until 1991.

United Nations

In 1945, 51 countries founded an organisation called the United Nations (UN). The UN works to help countries talk to each other and keep peace. There have been many wars since 1945, but no world war.

World War II facts and figures

Almost everything about World War II was newer, bigger, or different from before. Here are just a few facts about the biggest war in history.

During London air raids,

many families slept on Underground platforms.

Many people felt safer under ground.

The German V-2 rocket

flew so fast no one could hear it coming.

2 is the number of days a week Germans were allowed hot water for washing (they had to save fuel).

60,000,000

is the number of people believed to have died in World War II. This is more than in any other war.

US Marine Corps War Memorial

More than 100

British female pilots flew RAF planes from factories to airfields.

14

was the age of some German boy-soldiers in the final battles against the Allies.

In cinemas when an air raid began, a message on screen told people they could leave if they liked. Then the film went on.

Australians, like the British, planted Victory Gardens to grow more food.

50 vs 9

50 Nations fought on the Allied side, and 9 on the Axis side.

1,500,000

is the number of parts needed to build a Liberator bomber.

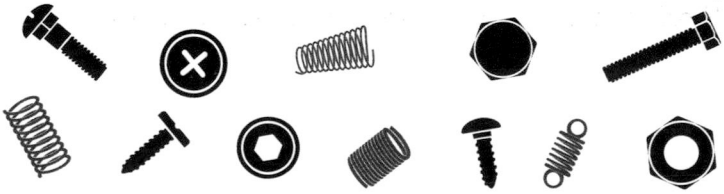

Glossary

Some words in the book may be new to you. This is what they mean. They will help you to learn about World War II.

aircraft carrier Huge ship with warplanes that fly to and from its flat deck

air raid Attack from the sky, by planes dropping bombs

Allies People who join in a shared aim. The main Allies in World War II were Britain, USA, France, and the Soviet Union (USSR)

atomic bomb Weapon using the power of split atoms to produce energy that destroys. Now called a nuclear weapon

Axis Nations on Germany's side in World War II, including Italy and Japan

battleship Large fighting ship, with big guns

blackout Ban on using lights in buildings at night so bombers couldn't spot them. People used thick curtains to hide light

Blitz Sudden, fast, and forceful air attack. From the German word *Blitzkrieg*, meaning "lightning war"

code Way to keep a message secret, by changing what it says. Knowing the code means someone can read it

Cold War The war without conflict that existed between the Soviet Union and USA following World War II

communism Way of life in which everything belongs to the state, or government. The wealth and products of the state are divided between its citizens, or people

People carried a gas mask, in case there was a gas attack.

concentration camp Place where people, mainly Jews, were kept prisoner in terrible conditions because of who they were. People in Nazi camps were used as slaves or killed

convoy Group of ships sailing together for safety

dogfight Close range battle between two aircraft

empire Group of countries conquered and then ruled over by one nation

evacuee Person moved from danger to a safer place, often from the city to the countryside

fascism Political movement that started in Italy. Fascists are against communism, and believe in their nation above all others. The Nazis in Germany were fascists

fighter plane Fast plane armed with guns

gas mask Goggle-like mask worn over the nose and mouth to protect people from breathing in poison gas

ghetto City area in which the Nazis forced Jews to live

grenade Small bomb thrown by a soldier

Holocaust The mass killing of 6 million Jews, and other groups of people, by the Nazis in World War II

invasion Going into an enemy's land with force

Jew Person whose own religion, or family religion, is Judaism

Kindertransport Train and ship journeys set up for some Jewish children to escape from the Nazis

landing craft Smaller boats used to take troops from big ships into shore

Luftwaffe Name of the German airforce

Morse code Code using dots and dashes for letters. Can be sent by flashing lights, by flags, or by long and short sounds

Nazi Member, or follower, of the Nazi Party (National Socialists) in Germany, led by Adolf Hitler

periscope Tube with mirrors that lets a submarine captain see what is above the water

propaganda Method used to change and control how people think and behave

propeller Spinning blades on an aircraft engine that move the plane

racism Thinking and acting against people of a different race because you believe you are better than them

radar Bouncing radio waves off an object to show where it is. Used to locate enemy aircraft and ships

rallies Huge meetings to get people excited. The Nazis used rallies to spread support in the 1930s

rationing Fixed amount of food and supplies. Used to ensure supplies are shared

refugee Person leaving home and going to another country to escape danger

Resistance Secret army working against Nazi occupiers in France, and other countries

siren Machine that makes a loud wailing sound to warn of a likely air raid

Soviet Union (USSR) "Union of Soviet Socialist Republics", a Russian-led communist group of countries that fought on the Allied side in the war

German tank

spy Person who gathers information in secret. In war, each side uses spies to find out the other's secrets

submarine Boat that can sail on the sea or dive to travel deep underwater

swastika Nazi sign or symbol, taken from an ancient cross with bent arms. In the past, it was a symbol of the sun and good luck

torpedo Weapon fired from a submarine. It travels underwater, hits a target, and explodes

torture Causing people pain, so that they will tell any secrets they know

U-boat German submarine

USSR See Soviet Union

war crime Action that breaks the laws or customs of warfare. Taking war criminals to court was new after World War II

Index

A

Afrika Korps 39
air raid wardens 50
air raids 10, 28, 29, 40, 50–51, 58
aircraft carriers 26
Allied powers 12, 13, 59
animals in war 28–29
atomic bomb 54–55
Auschwitz 34–35
Australia 13, 59
Axis powers 12, 59

B

B-29 bomber 55
Battle of Britain 20–21
Battle of the Bulge 52
Battle of Stalingrad 30–31
battleships 26–27, 43
Berlin Olympic Games 7, 23
Berlin Wall 57
Bismarck 26–27
blitzkrieg 11
bomber planes 4, 11, 20, 27, 32, 43, 59
boy soldiers 59
Britain 8, 9, 10, 13, 16–17, 28, 29, 44–45, 46–47, 56, 58

C

Canada 13
children 8–9, 24–25, 40, 41, 44, 45, 59
China 5, 13
Churchill, Winston 13, 17, 20
cinema 23, 24, 59
code breaking 46–47
Cold War 57
Colossus computer 47
concentration camps 34–35, 37
Condor bomber 27
Czechoslovakia 5, 9

D

D-Day landings 47, 48–49
death toll 58
desert warfare 38–39
Dornier DO 17 bomber 4
Douglas C-47 Skytrain 32
Dresden 50–51
DUKW amphibious vehicle 49
Dunkirk evacuation 16–17

E

Einstein, Albert 54
Enigma code machine 46
entertainment 23, 24–25
evacuees 8, 9, 40

F

farming 19, 40, 44, 45
Fermi, Enrico 55
fighter planes 20, 21, 32, 33
firebombs 50
flying boats 27
food supplies 19, 26, 40, 41, 44–45
France 11, 13, 14–15, 48–49, 52
Frank, Anne 36–37
French Resistance 15

G

gas masks 10, 40
German invasion 4, 10, 11, 13, 14–15, 30–31,
Germany 4, 11, 12, 13, 14–15, 30–31, 40, 41, 45, 46, 47, 50–51, 53, 58
grenades 31

H

Heinkel III bomber 20, 21
Hirohito, Emperor 12
Hiroshima 55
Hitler, Adolf 4, 5, 6, 10, 12, 16, 20, 21, 34, 40, 52, 53
Hitler Youth 40, 41
Holocaust 34–35
home front 18–19, 40–41, 44–45, 58
Hurricane fighter 21

I

Italy 5, 12

J

Japan 5, 12, 13, 26, 40, 42–43, 45, 55, 57
Jewish people 6, 7, 8–9, 34–37

K

Kawasaki Ki-100 fighter 33
Kindertransport 8–9
Kristallnacht 7

L

Lancaster bomber 32
Land Army 19

Liberator bomber 27, 59
Lorenz code machine 47
Luftwaffe 20, 21
Lynn, Vera 25
Lysander aircraft 15

M

Manhattan Project 54
medals 17, 28
Mein Kampf 6
memorials 35, 43, 55, 58
messenger pigeons 28, 29
Messerschmitt Me110 20
Messerschmitt Me262 33
mines 26, 28
Morse code 15, 47
Mosquito fighter/bomber 32
Moulin, Jean 15
Mussolini, Benito 5, 12

N

Nachthexen (Night Witches) 19
Nagasaki 55
naval warfare 26–27
Nazis 5, 6, 7, 22, 34, 35, 36, 37, 40-41, 57
Netherlands 11, 14, 36–37, 45, 52
New Zealand 13
newspapers 23
Night Witches 19
Normandy landings 48–49
North Africa 38–39
Norway 11, 14, 26
Nuremberg trials 57

O

Operation Dynamo 16–17
outbreak of war 10–11
Owens, Jesse 7

P

P-51 Mustang fighter 33
Panzer tank 4, 30–31
Pearl Harbor 12, 13, 42–43
pilots 19, 59
planes 4, 11, 20–21, 27, 32–33, 43, 59
Poland 4, 10, 14, 34
poppies 5
post-war world 56–57
pre-fabricated homes 56
prisoners of war 40
propaganda 22–23

R

radar 21
radio 23, 25
rationing 40, 44–45
Red Army 53
refugees 8–9, 11
Roosevelt, Franklin D. 13
Royal Air Force (RAF) 20, 21
Russia 13, 30–31

S

secret agents 15, 32, 47
Soviet Union (Russia) 13, 19, 30–31, 53, 56, 57
Spitfire fighter 21
Stalin, Joseph 13
Stalingrad 30–31
Station X (Bletchley Park) 46–47
submarines 26, 27
Sunderland flying boat 27

T

tanks 4, 11, 30–31, 53
torpedoes 17, 43
toys and games 24–25
transport planes 32
Turing, Alan 47

U

U-boats 27
United Nations (UN) 57
USA 12, 13, 19, 22, 26, 32, 33, 42–43, 45, 56, 57

V

V-1 flying bombs 52
V-2 rockets 52, 58
VE Day 53

W

war crimes 57
war work 10–19, 40, 41
warships 26, 27
Winton, Nicholas 9
women 18–19, 41, 59
World War I 4, 5, 6, 12
World War II 4–5, 10-11, 52–53, 58

World War II locations

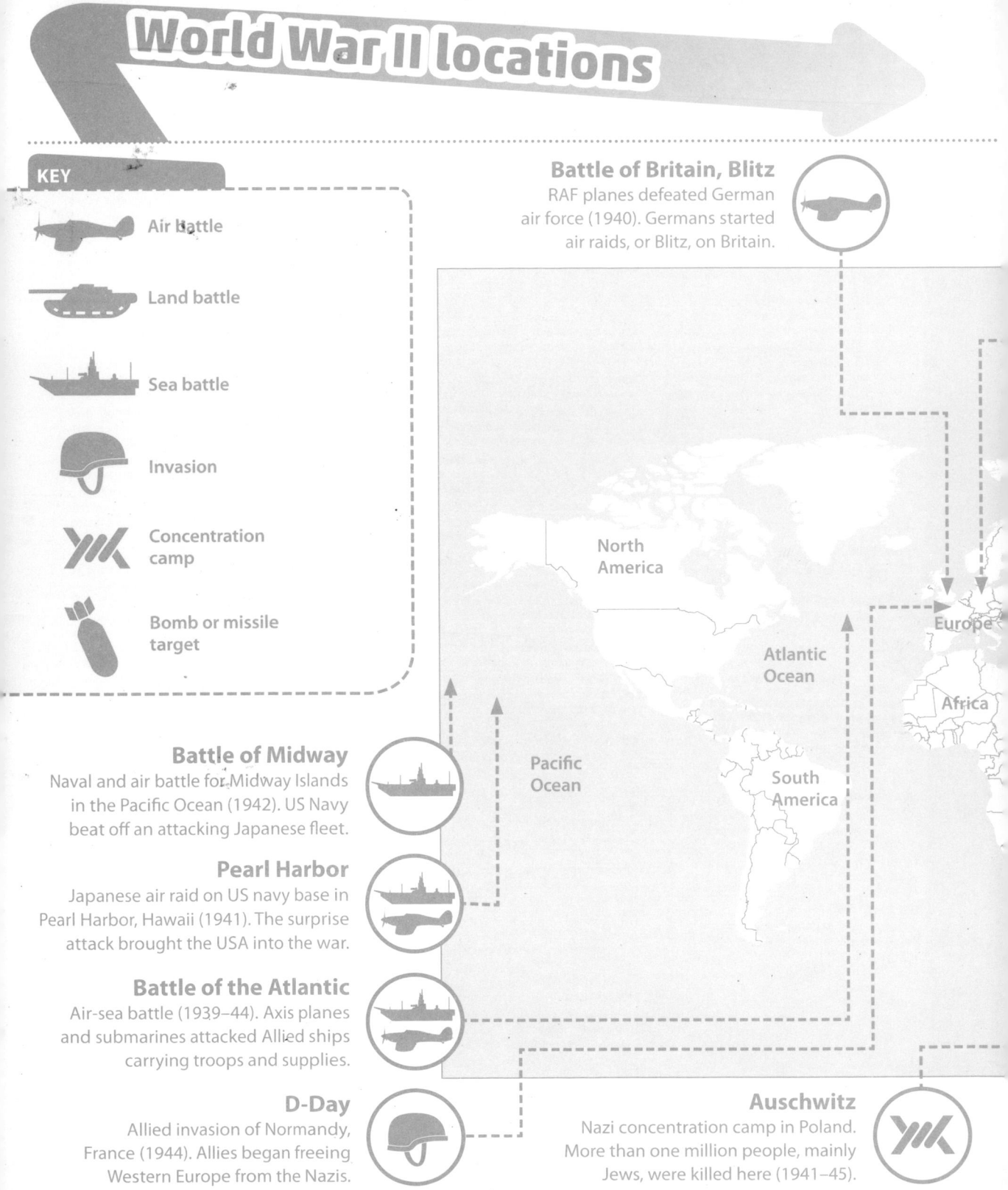